CD INCLUDED

ORCHESTRA PLAY-ALONG

POPULAR SONGS

CONTENTS

ISBN 978-1-4234-4573-9

HAL•LEONARD®
CORPORATION
7777 W. BLUEMOUND RD. P.O. BOX 13819 MILWAUKEE, WI 53213

T0056180

Visit Hal Leonard Online at
www.halleonard.com

From SWEET CHARITY
BIG SPENDER

VIOLIN

Music by CY COLEMAN
Lyrics by DOROTHY FIELDS
Arranged by ROBERT LONGFIELD

ELEANOR RIGBY

VIOLIN

Words and Music by JOHN LENNON
and PAUL McCARTNEY
Arranged by LARRY MOORE

Moderately, with a steady beat

From the Disney Channel Original Movie HIGH SCHOOL MUSICAL

HIGH SCHOOL MUSICAL
(Breaking Free • Start of Something New • We're All in This Together)

VIOLIN

Arranged by TED RICKETTS

Faster Rock "We're All in This Together"

From THE BODYGUARD

I WILL ALWAYS LOVE YOU

VIOLIN

Words and Music by
DOLLY PARTON
Arranged by ROBERT LONGFIELD

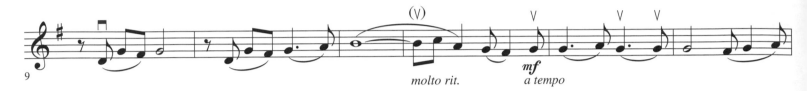

From SOPHISTICATED LADIES

IT DON'T MEAN A THING

(If It Ain't Got That Swing)

VIOLIN

Words and Music by DUKE ELLINGTON
and IRVING MILLS
Arranged by ROBERT LONGFIELD

From REQUIEM
PIE JESU

VIOLIN

By ANDREW LLOYD WEBBER
Arranged by JOHN LEAVITT

WE'VE ONLY JUST BEGUN

VIOLIN

Words and Music by ROGER NICHOLS
and PAUL WILLIAMS
Arranged by LARRY MOORE

From WHISTLE DOWN THE WIND

WHISTLE DOWN THE WIND

Violin

Music by ANDREW LLOYD WEBBER
Lyrics by JIM STEINMAN
Arranged by JOHN LEAVITT

This page has been left blank to facilitate page turns.

From SWEET CHARITY
BIG SPENDER

VIOLA

Music by CY COLEMAN
Lyrics by DOROTHY FIELDS
Arranged by ROBERT LONGFIELD

Moderate Swing

ELEANOR RIGBY

VIOLA

Words and Music by JOHN LENNON
and PAUL McCARTNEY
Arranged by LARRY MOORE

From the Disney Channel Original Movie HIGH SCHOOL MUSICAL

HIGH SCHOOL MUSICAL
(Breaking Free • Start of Something New • We're All in This Together)

VIOLA

Arranged by TED RICKETTS

BREAKING FREE
Words and Music by JAMIE HOUSTON
© 2005 Walt Disney Music Company
This arrangement © 2007 Walt Disney Music Company
All Rights Reserved   Used by Permission

START OF SOMETHING NEW • WE'RE ALL IN THIS TOGETHER
Words and Music by MATTHEW GERRARD and ROBBIE NEVIL
© 2005 Walt Disney Music Company
This arrangement © 2007 Walt Disney Music Company
All Rights Reserved   Used by Permission

VIOLA

"We're All in This Together"
Faster Rock

From THE BODYGUARD

I WILL ALWAYS LOVE YOU

VIOLA

Words and Music by
DOLLY PARTON
Arranged by ROBERT LONGFIELD

From SOPHISTICATED LADIES

IT DON'T MEAN A THING
(If It Ain't Got That Swing)

VIOLA

Words and Music by DUKE ELLINGTON
and IRVING MILLS
Arranged by ROBERT LONGFIELD

From REQUIEM
PIE JESU

VIOLA

By ANDREW LLOYD WEBBER
Arranged by JOHN LEAVITT

Andante espressivo

WE'VE ONLY JUST BEGUN

VIOLA

Words and Music by ROGER NICHOLS
and PAUL WILLIAMS
Arranged by LARRY MOORE

From WHISTLE DOWN THE WIND

WHISTLE DOWN THE WIND

VIOLA

Music by ANDREW LLOYD WEBBER
Lyrics by JIM STEINMAN
Arranged by JOHN LEAVITT

This page has been left blank to facilitate page turns.

From SWEET CHARITY
BIG SPENDER

Music by CY COLEMAN
Lyrics by DOROTHY FIELDS
Arranged by ROBERT LONGFIELD

CELLO

ELEANOR RIGBY

CELLO

Words and Music by JOHN LENNON
and PAUL McCARTNEY
Arranged by LARRY MOORE

From the Disney Channel Original Movie HIGH SCHOOL MUSICAL

HIGH SCHOOL MUSICAL

(Breaking Free • Start of Something New • We're All in This Together)

CELLO

Arranged by TED RICKETTS

CELLO

"We're All in This Together"

Faster Rock

From THE BODYGUARD

I WILL ALWAYS LOVE YOU

CELLO

**Words and Music by
DOLLY PARTON**
Arranged by ROBERT LONGFIELD

From SOPHISTICATED LADIES

IT DON'T MEAN A THING
(If It Ain't Got That Swing)

CELLO

Words and Music by DUKE ELLINGTON
and IRVING MILLS
Arranged by ROBERT LONGFIELD

From REQUIEM
PIE JESU

CELLO

By ANDREW LLOYD WEBBER
Arranged by JOHN LEAVITT

WE'VE ONLY JUST BEGUN

CELLO

Words and Music by ROGER NICHOLS
and PAUL WILLIAMS
Arranged by LARRY MOORE

From WHISTLE DOWN THE WIND

WHISTLE DOWN THE WIND

CELLO

Music by ANDREW LLOYD WEBBER
Lyrics by JIM STEINMAN
Arranged by JOHN LEAVITT

Moderato con moto expressivo

This page has been left blank to facilitate page turns.

From SWEET CHARITY
BIG SPENDER

Music by CY COLEMAN
Lyrics by DOROTHY FIELDS
Arranged by ROBERT LONGFIELD

Bass

ELEANOR RIGBY

Words and Music by JOHN LENNON
and PAUL McCARTNEY
Arranged by LARRY MOORE

Bass

From the Disney Channel Original Movie HIGH SCHOOL MUSICAL

HIGH SCHOOL MUSICAL

(Breaking Free • Start of Something New • We're All in This Together)

BASS

Arranged by TED RICKETTS

BASS

"We're All in This Together"
Faster Rock

From THE BODYGUARD

I WILL ALWAYS LOVE YOU

BASS

Words and Music by
DOLLY PARTON
Arranged by ROBERT LONGFIELD

From SOPHISTICATED LADIES

IT DON'T MEAN A THING
(If It Ain't Got That Swing)

Bass

Words and Music by DUKE ELLINGTON
and IRVING MILLS
Arranged by ROBERT LONGFIELD

From REQUIEM
PIE JESU

BASS

By ANDREW LLOYD WEBBER
Arranged by JOHN LEAVITT

WE'VE ONLY JUST BEGUN

Words and Music by ROGER NICHOLS
and PAUL WILLIAMS
Arranged by LARRY MOORE

Bass

WHISTLE DOWN THE WIND

Bass

Music by ANDREW LLOYD WEBBER
Lyrics by JIM STEINMAN
Arranged by JOHN LEAVITT